THE ADVENTURES OF

MOLI AND CULE

A true to life story for children of all ages

by Jeri L. Berc, Ph.D.

Dedicated to carrying on the spirit and energy of Rachel Carson

To Rosie,
Happy Adventures!

Jeri B

A Note About the Book

All of the Adventures in this book are of biological, chemical, and physical entities and processes. It is not necessary, however, to identify to the reader what they all are in technical terms. Familiarity with the story, though, should facilitate learning about these processes in more traditional educational approaches. A glossary is provided at the end of the text with the technical names of the processes and entities. The goal of the book is not only to ease the learning of the science, but to instill a sense of caring in the reader for the entities and processes described. It is not geared to any specific age of reader, though it can be appreciated by imaginative and curious children in a wide span of ages. New meanings in the text emerge as the reader matures.

About the author

After completing a BA in Social Sciences from the University of Michigan, Jeri Berc studied landscaping and soil science with the goal to be a scientist for sustainable agriculture. She earned a BA in biology from San Francisco State University and a MS and PH.D. in Soil Science from the University of California at Berkeley. She worked in the USDA Natural Resources Conservation Service on sustainable agriculture, soil quality, and ecosystem based management of agricultural land and retired after contributing to United Nations negotiations on climate change, desertification, biodiversity, and sustainable development. Since retiring she has developed a small scale sustainable farm which includes horses, chickens and bees along with flowering meadows, hay, fruit and annual crops. Her goal is to establish a vocational education institute on her farm in sustainable agriculture and to provide a showcase for sustainable land use in a suburban setting.

Gratitudes:

To Linn Shapiro for editing. To Connie Gersick for saving, unearthing, and returning the long lost manuscript to me. To Troy Gaines who painted the cover art, Enchanted Forest. To the Passion Works Studio, in Athens Ohio, dedicated to collaborative work between artists with and without developmental disabilities. To my teachers at San Francisco State University who taught me all the science in this book.

All proceeds from the sale of this book shall be donated to non-profit organizations, including the Passion Works Studio.

The Adventures of Moli and Cule

I.

It's the end of the summer and the apples are full grown. Soon they'll be leaving their Mother Tree.

"I hope I get picked and eaten," said Delicious Apple. "I'd like to join an animal. Then I can travel and see new places."

"I want to find a home," said the Little Baby Seed inside Delicious. "and grow up into a new apple tree."

Red Apple was scared. He trembled on his branch.

"Aren't you afraid, Baby Seed? You might be chewed up. How do you know what it's like inside an animal, Delicious? What if you want to get out and you can't? I want to drop and rot into the earth. I want to grow into an apple again next year."

"If you keep shaking like that," Delicious warned, "you'll drop to the ground right now."

Thud! Red's stem shook free of the branch. He landed on the soft ground below the apple tree. At the edge of the meadow stood Big Deer. She listened for danger but heard only bees and birds. She sniffed the air and smelled only apples. Big Deer pranced into the meadow. She jumped against the apple tree, rested her front legs on the trunk, stretched her neck, and closed her teeth around an apple. Big Deer had eaten Delicious Apple with Little Baby Seed inside!

II.

Little Baby Seed found herself in a dark cave. Clear juices poured into the cave. A soft red floor moved up and down. Rows of giant pillars crushed the apple between them. Little Baby Seed tried to swim away from the pillars but the moving floor pushed her back.

"Delicious, what is happening?" she cried.

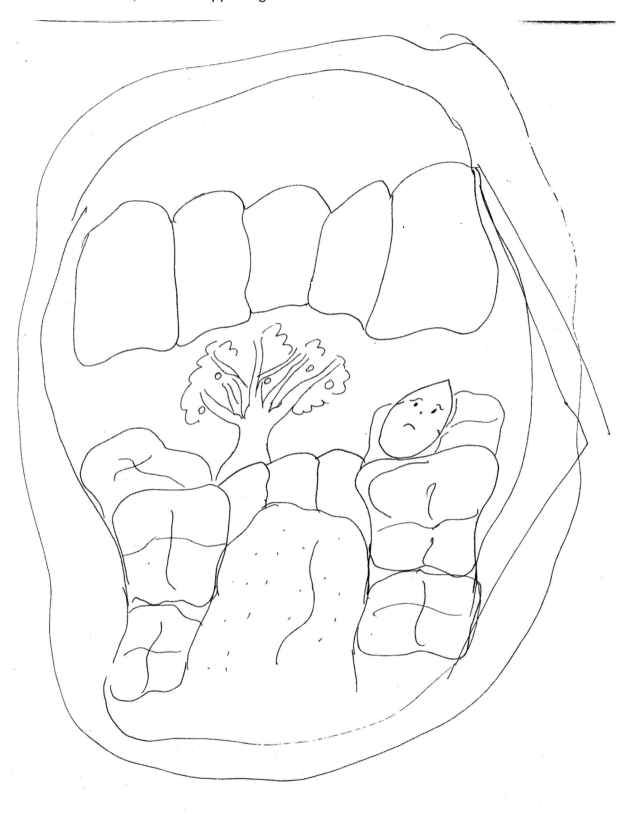

Delicious called back, "I'm getting chewed into chunks. I was such a nice big apple, but this is the only way for me to travel."

The moving floor pushed Little Baby Seed onto a pillar. Another pillar came down on top of her but it did not crush her. The soft, moving floor swept her with the juices and the chunks of Delicious Apple through a small dark tunnel into a large hole. More juices gushed in from all sides. Soft walls squished in and out. The chunks of Delicious Apple were melting into the bubbling juices.

"What's happening to you now?" cried Little Baby Seed.

One little chunk answered, "We are changed. Before we were Delicious Apple. Now we are tiny apple bits. We are small so it's hard to see us. But we are still here. And we are still sweet. We are Sweet Apple Tiny Bits. Soon you won't see us at all. The pillars and juices made us small enough to squeeze through the walls. We are joining Big Deer's blood on the other side of the wall. Goodbye!"

Little Baby Seed was glad that the pillars had not crushed her to bits. She thanked her mother tree for her heavy coat that protected her from the juices. Getting smashed to bits was all right for Delicious who wanted to become part of an animal, but Little Baby Seed wanted to be herself. She wanted to grow into a new apple tree. The squishing walls pushed her on. Little Baby Seed was caught in a gooey mush.

"How do you do?" said the mush. "I am Mana Ure. I used to be baby seeds like you and other things like twigs and stems. I got crushed between the white pillars. My parts were too big, though, to go with Sweet Apple Tiny Bits into Big Deer's blood. We are now in the last tunnel."

Pinch! The last tunnel squeezed Little Baby Seed and then let go. She flew out of the tunnel and landed on the green grass. All was still. The squishing, churning, pushing, heaving and flying stopped. Little Baby Seed was safe on the ground inside Mana Ure. She fell into a deep sleep. Through the long winter, Mana Ure protected Little Baby Seed. He was soft and warm and the winds could not get through him. Winter turned to spring.

One morning, an earthworm gobbled up Little Baby Seed and Mana Ure. They were soon pushed out of the earthworm into the underground. It started to rain. Mana Ure melted away and slid deeper underground.

As he left, he called back, "When you are ready to grow, break out of your old coat. Then I'll come back to you through your new roots."

As she got warmer and wetter, Little Baby Seed felt a stirring inside. A crack in her coat opened and out popped a root pipe. It grew down, sucking water into her from the ground below. She swelled with the water and from the crack in her coat, a stem pushed out and up. It grew towards the sky, taller and taller. Her roots dug deeper and deeper. They found Mana Ure and sucked him in to feed her. Her first leaves unfolded. Little Baby Seed looked up and down proudly. She was growing into an apple tree.

III.

Sweet Apple Tiny Bits did not sleep that winter. They passed through the holes of the long, narrow tunnel into Big Deer's blood. The Pro Team Tricycle Riders greeted them.

"We will carry you about in Big Deer's blood. But this is no free ride. We will take you to work in the Mighty Condra's Tricycle Factories throughout Big Deer. When you have repaired all the tricycles that you can, the Pro Team Tricycle Riders will pick you up and take you to the Activity Directors, R 'n A. They will assign you to your next job."

The Pro Team Tricycle Riders loaded Sweet Apple Tiny Bits onto their tricycles. The veins and arteries of the blood stream ran every which way. The Bits saw from the outside the tunnels they had passed through earlier. Tricycle riders raced around the tunnels making them squish in and out. Others carried buckets of the juices that had melted them into bits.

All that racing wore out the tricycles. Quite often, a Team member carried a tricycle to a repair factory inside a house on the side of the roadway. It picked up a new tricycle and went back to the races on the tunnel.

As the caravan of Bits travelled, their Pro Team drivers called out, "Fresh SATBs (that's short for Sweet Apple Tiny Bits) here. Get them while they last."

The Mighty Condra called back, "Stop here, SATB needed."

Without another word, one of the Team would pass a Bit in to the tricycle factory.

They soon left the long tunnels and came to a giant scissor. Attached to the scissor were the giant white pillars.

"This is where we came in to Big Deer," said one Tiny Bit!

"But it's not where we're leaving," added another.

They rode on and found themselves inside two delicate pipes. Wind whooshed in and out.

"Where are we?" asked one Bit.

"I know, it's the nose!" exclaimed another.

In the nose were the Professional Team members. There weren't many of them. They wore white coats and carried little bottles. Each bottle was opened and put into a hole in a nose pipe. The Professional Team member would then sniff the air in the bottle and label it: Apples, Grass, Water, Danger: Smoke. Making sure the bottle was tightly corked, the Team member would send it along with a Pro Team Driver.

"What are you doing?" asked one Sweet Apple Tiny Bit.

"I am testing the air around the nose," answered the Professional. "I name the scents and send them to the brain. The brain sends messages to the body. Danger messages are most important. If I pick up a scent of Danger, like Smoke, I send it up to the brain as fast as the fastest Pro Team member can ride. The brain sends a message to the legs: 'Run!' Even if I smell an apple while we're running, we won't stop to eat until I send 'Smoke Clear' messages to the brain."

Some of the Apple Bits stayed to work with the Professionals. The remaining Bits moved along.

They saw more Pro Team Tricycle Riders open two huge window shades. The Sweet Apple

Tiny Bits gasped. Through two round windows they saw their mother apple tree.

Little Bits see their apple tree when the window shades are raised.

13

Then the shades dropped and it was dark again as the caravan continued. They came upon a drum skin stretched over a hollow tube.

"We are the Reverse Musicians," said a Team member working there. We listen to what is being played on the drum skin and write it down."

"What makes the drum play?" questioned one Tiny Bit.

"Everything in the world which makes a sound causes vibrations to wave through the air. When those sound waves hit this drum, the vibrations make the drum sing. Every vibration is different and makes the drum sing a different song. From the song, we can tell what in the outside world made the sound. That is what we write down. We send that to the brain with a Pro Team Tricycle Rider. The brain figures out where to send the messages so the Big Deer can do the right thing."

Suddenly a thunderous explosion filled the chamber. The drum skin waved violently back and forth. "Danger: Gun Shot," wrote a Reverse Musician, and a Pro Team Tricycle Rider raced it to the brain.

"Hold on! We'll be moving fast", warned the Reverse Musician. Another crashing explosion filled the tunnel as the Sweet Apple Tiny Bits started flying in all directions.

"We're getting in the way here," said one Pro Team Driver. "We'll go up to the brain to get directions. We're surely needed someplace else."
The brain looked like a spider in her web. Driving on the webbed paths, Pro Team Drivers approached the spider brain from all directions.

The spider said, "Leave some Apple Bits here. Then go to the lungs, the heart, and the legs. Hurry! We are in danger."
The Drivers lost no time. They followed the nose pipe into the lung. Air rushed in and out. Some Bits stayed to work. The rest went with the Pro Team Drivers to the

pulsating heart and those left raced to the tricycle factories of the hard–working leg muscles. One last little Bit remained. She rode to Big Deer's tail.

"End of the line," called the Pro Team Driver. "Off you go. You will help the tail twitch."

IV.

The Last Little Bit thought back on her amazing journey through Big Deer: tricycles riding here and there, pushing and pulling, delivering messages, juices, and little bits like herself. But she missed light and air. The Last Little Bit wanted a position on the outside. If she worked hard, perhaps she could go outside.

A Pro Team Driver came out of a house and said, "Are you ready to meet the Mighty Condra of the Tail? He has a backlog of tricycles and he needs help."

"I am ready," replied the Last Little Bit.

The Pro Team Driver carried her into a house filled with creatures and compartments. Everything was floating in jelly. Some of the creatures were holding up the walls.

"Who is in charge? Please take me to the Directors," said the Last Little Bit.

"No time to stop," said the Pro Team Driver. "You are needed in the factory."

Inside the tricycle factory, a deep booming voice called to her, "Well, a fresh Sweet Apple Tiny Bit. I am Mighty Condra. I will show you how this factory works and teach you to make the tricycles that the Pro Team Drivers ride."

Spare tires rolled onto a work bench. The Little Bit tightened the bolts which kept the tires

attached to the tricycles.   Alone, the Last Little Bit worked hard and dreamed of the outside.

Time passed. The Little Bit did not know if it was day or night. In the dimly-lit factory, there was no

morning, no mid-day sun, no dusk. She saw only tricycles rolling off her bench. She had done her

best and now began to get tired. The tricycles rolled away slower and slower. Finally, she could

not go on. The Last Little Bit rested her head on her work bench. She dreamed of the smell of the earth, the feel of the wind, and the color of the blue sky.

Sweet apple tiny bits
working in the Mighty Condra's Tricycle Factory

"Reached your limit, eh?" Mighty Condra boomed.

"I'll have the Pro Team drivers carry you to R 'n A, the Activity Directors. They'll give you your next task. Someone with work left in them will take your place."

R 'n A were coiled together, their long, waving bodies wound around each other. As the Last Little Bit approached, R 'n A straightened up.

"Come here, Little Bit," they ordered. R 'n A rubbed their bodies against the Bit, all the while talking to themselves. "Not bad here. Don't know what we can use this for. This will do nicely...."

"Urgent Message! " A Pro Team Messenger rushed up. "Cold outside: do something!"

"What do we do?" R whispered to A. "I can't remember what to do when it gets cold."

"We'd better get in touch with D 'n A. They made everyone. They always know what to do." said A.

R 'n A called for a Pro Team messenger. "Go to the inner chamber where our folks, D 'n A, live. Ask them what we do when it gets cold."

The Pro Team messenger rode to D 'n A's special inner chamber along webs in the jelly. The walls of the chamber were ringed with Pro Tectors. The Pro Team messenger passed the message from R 'n A to a gate keeper in the Pro Tector ring who returned quickly with a response. The Messenger pedaled back to R 'n A.

As soon as R 'n A got the message, they looked at the Last Little Bit and said, "We need a new winter coat. You are going to become fur."

"You mean I'm going outside? That's just what I wanted! Thank you so much." The Little Bit grabbed R 'n A and hugged them tightly.

"Now, now, Little Bit. Neither you nor we had anything to do with this decision. It is what is needed and what you can do. Away you go. Don't get too cold out there. It's going to be a long winter."

The Last Little Bit jumped on to a waiting tricycle and called gleefully, "Thank you. Thank you all. I'm on my way to the world outside!"

Nobody paid much attention to her. Mighty Condra kept working in his tricycle factory. The Pro Team Tricycle Riders kept riding on the webs through the jelly. R 'n A were tied up with each other again. The Pro Tectors around D 'n A did not open a clasped hand to wave goodbye. The Pro Team Driver carried the Last Little Bit to the outer edge of the house. There another driver waited to take her through the wall into the outside air.

V.

Coming into the air, the Little Bit blinked her eyes, adjusting to the bright light. Her beautiful world: blue sky, golden sun, green plants, and the brown earth below. Now she could see it and smell it. She could even touch it when Big Deer rubbed against grass or trees. Looking around, the Last Little Bit recognized other Tiny Bits from Delicious Apple. They were coming out as fur from other houses inside Big Deer. Though they looked different, they were somehow familiar to each other. They had a bit reunion. The new winter fur coat waved together, happy in the autumn breeze.

The meadow looked different too. Red and yellow leaves floated to the ground. Apples, left on their old tree, on the highest branches out of Big Deer's reach, were dull brown. So were the few which remained on the ground. They were mushy and melting into the earth. The Little Bits of Fur remembered Red Apple on the ground. They called to him but heard no reply.

Big Deer lay down to rest. The Fur rubbed into the ground. The earth was warm and soft. The wind could not chill them. They snuggled together to rest. Nights and days passed. Big Deer roamed from the early morning light until the last rays blinked through the forest. Each day was shorter than the one before. The nights became longer and colder. Snow covered the land. The Little Bits of Fur huddled together to keep warm.

One night when they had just fallen asleep, the voice of a New Deer woke them. "Is that you, my deer?" whispered the voice.

"Of course," came the answer. "I know that you are a deer. Do you not know me? Come closer to me and let your senses tell you."

"I must be sure," the New Deer explained. He crouched and came forward cautiously. "Smelling your deer scents and rubbing your deer fur, I do know. You are a deer. Truly, my deer. Just like me. Just for me. A deer."

The Little Bits of fur were proud to be admired. They stood up straight, only to be mussed by the fur of New Deer. The two deer spent many nights together. Through the cold winter, they kept each other warm.

VI

At last the days grew longer. The afternoon sun burned higher in the sky, brighter and stronger each day. The snow melted and disappeared from the ground. Big Deer's winter coat became too hot and heavy for her. One day she rubbed fur off on to the trunk of the old Mother Apple

20

Tree. As the bits of fur floated to the ground they wondered where they would go. One bit wept as she hit the ground.

Another asked, "What is your name, why are you crying."

"My name is Moli and I am tired of all these adventures. I want to be back up on a nice sunny branch in our old tree. I'm afraid to go underground."

"Don't be afraid Moli. My name is Cule. I'll stay with you. You can count on me."
Moli took Cule's hand and dried her tears just as an earthworm gobbled them up. They were squished into a small tunnel and were showered with white juices.

"You're turning frosty white." Moli said.

"You are too." Cule replied, as they were cast out underground by the hungry earthworm who returned to the surface for more fresh bits.

Underground, Moli and Cule were surrounded by yellow, blue, black, and glittering crystals. Pools of water lined the sides of the crystals. They decided to go for a swim. Other bits of fur, also cast underground by the earthworm, joined them in the pools. They were having such a good time

21

laughing and splashing they did not hear the first drops of the spring rain.

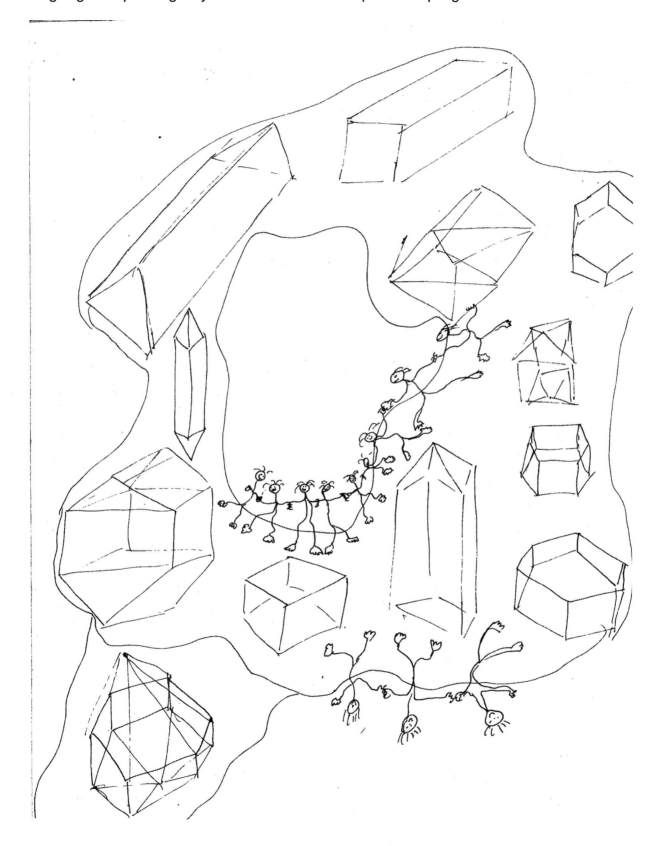

VII.

The sunlight glistening through the crystals dimmed. Thunder rumbled above. Trickles of rain turned to a full flow sweeping the little bits deeper underground. They clung together in fear. Clumped, they could hold fast to the edges of crystals. They rested against the pull of the water in the cracks between the crystals. At last the flood ceased. The little bits sighed in relief and the invasion of the colonial animalcule armies began.

VIII.

Round ones popped out of tiny specks. Spirally ones squiggled in through the cracks between the crystals. Some had long tails that whipped them about.

One called to another, "Nitro, some tender bits for you here."

"Thanks Actin, very good old boy. Nothing here for Sal, pity."

"Well, let's move along now."

The little bits were gobbled up and expelled before they could be afraid. They found themselves changed into new clothes. As the little bits looked themselves over, a root pipe burrowed into the crystal crack next to them.

A Pro Team Driver popped his head out of a hole in the root and called to the little bits, "All aboard, going up to the top of Mother Apple Tree."

He dropped a vacuum pump into a pool which sucked up the water. The little bits flowed into the pipe. They were joyful to reunite with their old tree.

As they rode up, the Pro Team Driver explained, "We are going to the beautiful Island Green Leaf. There is much work to be done. We need workers for Chloro and Phyll's Sugar Factories. We need Guards for the doors, and Pro Team Messengers and Drivers. Some of you may join R 'n A, some may become a part of D 'n A. Think about what you want to do and when we arrive, the Activity Directors, R 'n A will assign you to positions."

IX

One curious bit watched the water flow up and wondered what pulled it up and where it poured out. She thought if she became an activity director she would find out how everything worked. She decided to join R 'n A. Another more philosophic bit wanted to be away from the hustle and bustle of daily life so she could learn ancient knowledge, wisdom and truth. She chose to join D 'n A. Moli and Cule wanted to stick together. They thought it would be too much thinking to join D 'n A and too much responsibility to join R 'n A. They figured working in Chloro and Phyll's Sugar Factory would be light and sweet. That was their decision, they would work in a Sugar Factory. The Last Little Bit wanted to travel about on the Island, so decided to become a Pro Team Driver. Another Bit chose to be a Guard. Most of the Bits had their minds made up when they arrived at their new home.

X.

Sunlight filtered through green windows everywhere, and streams of water made the island a paradise. R 'n A greeted them and assigned them to their positions. They were all off to their new jobs, happy and content. The curious Bit became Professor U of R 'n A. The philosophic Bit became Sage T of D 'n A. Moli and Cule went to work in Chloro and Phyll's Sugar factory, and

the Last Little Bit become a Pro Team Driver riding a tricycle all over the Island. Professor U a

beginning student, was eager to learn how the Activity Directors worked. R was very long and A

was very short.

R began the lesson. "My body knows how to build. Everything is built from a chain of

four types of building blocks, each in its own special order. My body is a long chain of

these building blocks, with the order for everything else built into different parts of the

chain. If we need something built,   A finds free blocks and bits that match them and

links them to the place in my body that has the order for the thing that we need. That is all

we do. Once something has its blocks and bits lined up in the right order, it takes its form all by

itself, and is ready to do its job. If we don't know what to build, we send a messenger to D

'n A, and they tell us where on my body to begin the thing that is needed. If this is clear,

Professor U, now join A.

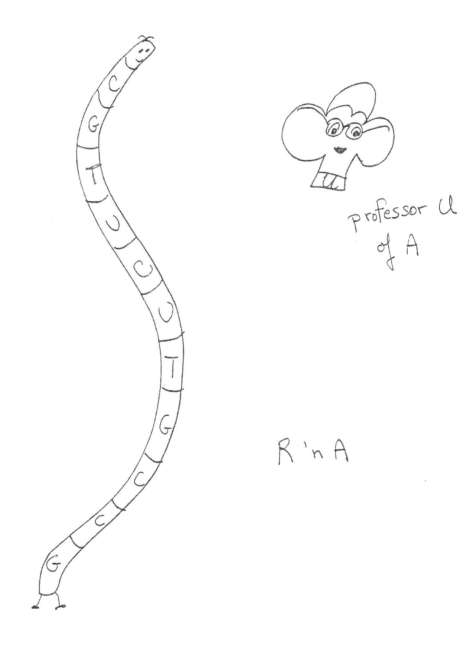

professor U
of A

R'n A

The Professor wondered how it could all be so simple and went to work thinking, "being is knowing, or is it knowing is being?"

D'nA

The little Bit who chose to become a guard went to her post where she was greeted by an old guard standing across the doorway.

"Hello", he said, "my name is Red. What's your name, where did you come from?"

"I'm Delicious, a Bit of Delicious Apple, I used to be in Big Deer's winter fur."

"What a small world." Red exclaimed. "I am a bit of Red, the apple who hung next to you when you were an apple too. How was it inside Big Deer?"

"It was quite interesting, and a great delight to see all the pretty land when I was fur outside." Red shivered at the thought. "I am glad to be back though, this is my favorite place."

"I agree, I never want to leave." said Red.

"Now, you must learn your new job. Look outside, what do you see?"

"Nothing, just air." replied the Delicious guard.

"You must look more closely. There is Magic Fairy Dust, COO COOs, OO OOs and HHO HHOs."

"I'm not CooCoo or OO OO and who's a hho hho" said Delicious indignantly.

"I know", replied Red, "Those are some of the creatures in the Magic Fairy Dust. COO COO's come in the door and go to Chloro and Phyll's factory where they are made into sugar. Then OO OOs come out of the factory and leave through our door. HHO HHOs, who used to be plain water in the streams also leave. Can you see them all, dancing about in the air?"

Delicious looked more carefully and finally could see the little creatures swirling and twirling in what she had thought was thin air.

"Yes I can see them!" she chirped gleefully.

"Very good." Red continued. "All we have to do is let them pass in and out. If it gets too hot or windy for the Sugar Factory to work, we close the door. When the factory shuts down at night, we close the door too. So stand up proud, swell up your chest, this is a very important job, and that is all we have to do."

"Snack time" called the Last Little Bit, who was now a Pro Team Driver, as she approached the Guards.

"Goodie!" said Red, "We need nourishment to do our job."

"Sugar, fresh from the sugar factory and Special K Bits from underground", said the Last Pro Team Driver.

"Thanks" said the Guards as they ate up their food, swelling their
bellies along with their chests.

31

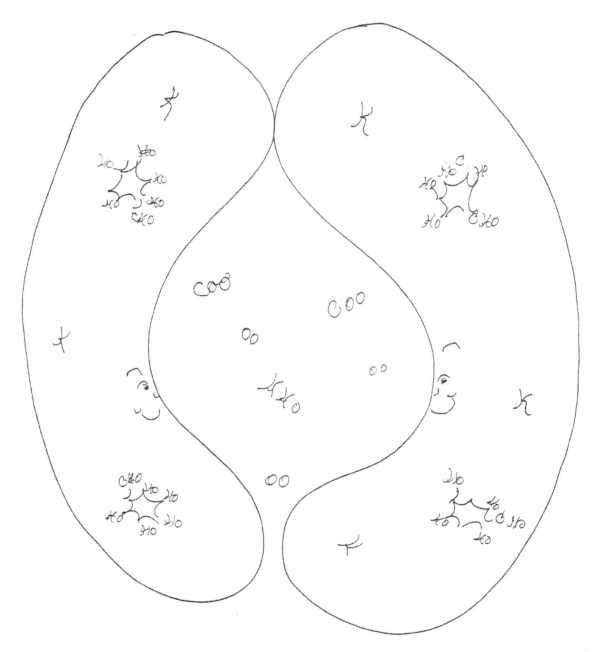

The guards at the door, full of sugar
and K bits.

XII.

Just as the Last Tricycle Driver left to bring snacks to the other Guards on the Island, Professor U arrived at Red and Delicious Guards' Door.

"Hello," she said, "I am investigating the flow of water and I've traced the streams to this door. The water flows upward through the apple tree and the stream stops here. What do you make of it? What pulls the water up here to the top of our tree? Where does the water go from here? How does it disappear?"

Red had been watching his door for a long time and knew the answer at once.

"It's simple, HHO used to be plain water. HHO joins the magic fairy dust at our door and dances out into the air."

"Who used to be water? Magic fairy dust? Dancing? I don't understand a bit of what you are saying. I don't see anything leaving the gate."
Professor U was confused.

"Professor, you must look more closely at the air." The Delicious guard tried to help. "There is magic fairy dust in it. HHO is one of the fairies. HHO used to be plain water but jumped out to twirl and swirl free in the air."

The professor looked more carefully. "Oh yes!" she exclaimed, "now I see them, little water creatures, HHOsies, jumping out of the water. Look at all of them in the water, there are millions and millions of them. They're all holding hands. Why they're holding on to the sides of the streams and climbing up the banks. They're all pulling each other out here. They must just love to dance free in the air because they all seem to be pulling themselves up here to do it. I never noticed them before in the air because, alone, they are so small. You just have to look more closely. How wonderful. Well, goodbye now. I hear Sage T of D 'n A calling me in to the inner chamber."

XIII.

In the inner chamber with D 'n A, Sage T wished to be enlightened. But she did not understand the nature of light.

Whenever she asked about it, what she heard sounded like nonsense, "light is knowing, and knowing is being, so light is being."

She needed to contact the outside world to understand reality. She called her old friend from Delicious Apple, Professor U. When the Professor arrived she explained her question.

Professor U suggested, "There is more light in Chloro and Phyll's Sugar Factories than anywhere else on the island. I will go and find Moli and Cule in their factory and see if they can help us solve this problem of the nature of light."

XIV.

Professor U arrived at Chloro and Phyll's Sugar Factory where Moli and Cule worked. Green light poured out of the door when Chloro and Phyll greeted the Professor. They were Green Lovers. They were completely green and everything in their factory was green.

"Hello", Chloro said, "What can we do for you?"

"I would like to speak with my friends Moli and Cule. I am studying light for Sage T of D 'n A."

"Yes, come right in," Phyll continued, "Moli and Cule are just inside.

Moli and Cule were tossing glowing light balls about. Bits of sugar were dancing around them.

"Hello my friends, can you explain light to me. How does it make things be?"

Moli began to explain, "The light balls are so beautiful we get excited just playing with them. We can't help laughing and dancing. This work is fun. The COO COOs, in the Magic Fairy Dust, feel the same way."

Cule continued, "They join hands in little groups and laugh and dance together. They only drink a bit of water. Six C's stick together, always laughing, HO HO. The 00's drop out of the ring and leave. That's how sugar is made from light."

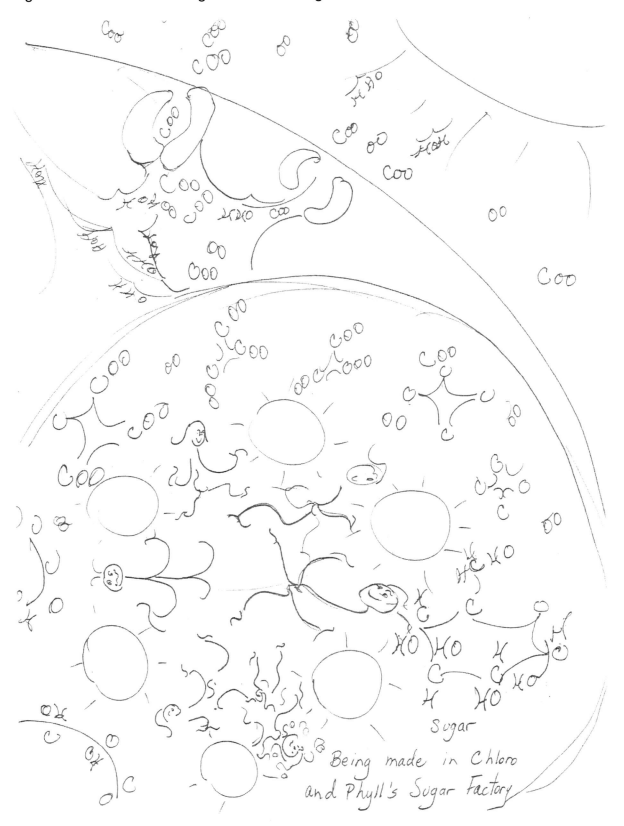

Sugar

Being made in Chloro
and Phyll's Sugar Factory

The professor was so elated, she started to dance herself.

"I see the light", she said. "I must go now and tell Sage T all about it."
Professor U passed into the inner chamber.

Sage T greeted her, "What news do you bring?"

"Light is balls of light that Moli and Cule toss about. The light balls are very exciting to the COO COOs and they join hands laughing and dancing. The 00's drop out of the ring, the C's stick together laughing, HO HO, and that is how sugar is made."

"The energy we get when we eat sugar is from light, eh? So light is being sometime after all. Very exciting." Sage T concluded. "You must get back to work now. It's flower time."

XV.

"Flower time!" the Professor announced to R 'n A when she returned to her work site.

Fresh bits were arriving from underground and sugar was being sent in from the factories. They were getting linked together by the activity directors to make parts for their flower. Tricycle drivers carried the bits and pieces to the tiny flower bud just above the island. The bud grew. Everyone on the island stopped to admire their creation when the flower opened its petals and released its scent. Flowers opened throughout the tree. Honey bees buzzed from flower to flower sucking the sweet nectars.

The Last Tricycle Driver was delivering the Last Little Bit of nectar to the flower when she met a lovely new creature perched on a stalk inside the flower.

"Hello" he said, "my name is Polli. Thanks for the nectar. It brings to me my magic carpet, the honey bee."

"Where do you go on your magic carpet?" asked the Driver.

"We fly into all the beautiful flowers we can find. When I find the most irresistible, I jump in, and there is love inside."

"What is love?" asked the Driver.

"I cannot explain love, but it is the most special feeling in the world." Just then a honey bee landed in the flower. "Here's my ride. Farewell."

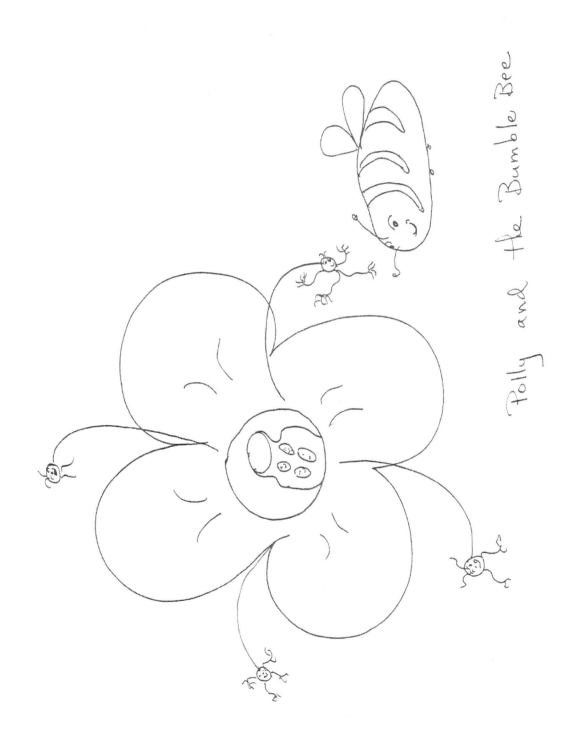

Polly and the Bumble Bee

The Last Driver waved goodbye and thought, "I want to be Polli. I want to ride the honey bee, visit the flowers, and find love. I will request that job next year," she decided as she went back to her work.

The flower's petals eventually faded and dropped to the ground. Only the center of the flower remained. The Last Driver delivered sugar and other bits to this core. It grew big and round. The driver soon realized it was a new apple. Big Deer came into the meadow with a new fawn to look at the young apples. Her mouth watered, but she knew she had to wait until they were big and red. There was plenty of grass and leaves to eat in the meantime. The little bits of Delicious apple were glad to see Big Deer with a new fawn. They hoped she would eat the new apple they were busy growing.

XVI.

Whoosh!

The little bits could not watch the deer anymore because a strange flying creature landed on the island. He stuck his needle mouth into the leaf and began to suck up the sugar the Pro Team Drivers were carrying to the apple. The drivers raced to R 'n A for help.

"What will we do? Our apple will never be sweet for Big Deer if this flying creature sucks up all of our sugar!"

R 'n A were stumped. They sent a message to D 'n A. The reply came quickly.

"It is A Fid, a common insect. Easily removed with anti-A Fid scent number 335."

R 'n A immediately located order number 335. They assembled the brew and turned it over to a Pro Team Driver. The Driver rode it to the A Fid's nose and poured it out. The A Fid's nose twitched. He pulled his needle out of the leaf.

"Ha Choo, Ha Choo", he sneezed and flew away.

All the little bits cheered, "Hooray!" for their victory.

XVII.

Their celebration, though, was short lived. A giant flying creature buzzed overhead. It dipped down over the forest. Clouds of smoke billowed from its wings. The dust settled in the forest. They heard wailing cries from the forest. The meadow was suddenly filled with animals racing from the woods.

"It's Herbie Cide!" a bird choked while resting on a branch of the apple tree. "He kills everything!"

"I will live!" cried out the Mother Apple Tree, as all the little bits spoke together in one deep voice.

The wind picked up and the dust drifted to the Apple tree. D 'n A got the message at once. All of the doors were ordered shut. Herbie Cide landed on the leaves. He laughed at the guards holding each other, tightly barring the doors.

"You'll get tired soon enough, then I'll get in and have what I want in your little island."

The whole day the doors remained closed. Magic Fairy Dust stayed outside with Herbie Cide. Water did not flow. No sugar was made. All were still, waiting. The next morning everyone was hungry and thirsty.

D 'n A said, "We must work, we must eat and drink or we will die. Open the doors."

As soon as the doors cracked open, Herbie Cide rushed in. He grabbed onto R 'n A's back and would not let go. D 'n A sent out repair crews. It was useless. When they freed R 'n A in one place, Herbie Cide grabbed another place. D 'n A ordered the doors shut. It was too late. Herbie Cide broke through the Pro Tector ring into the inner chamber. They grabbed D 'n A's back and would not let go. The doors to the Island Green Leaf never opened again.

XVIII.

The Island Leaf shriveled and dried up. The Little Bits wept as they floated to the ground. Cule tried to comfort Moli.

"Do not despair. Look, our leaf has sheltered other leaves from Herbie Cide. They are still alive. We can come back and work in another sugar factory next year. We are still together and our tree is alive."

They were both thankful for that as they settled to the ground. Earthworms brought the Little Bits underground as men came to the forest to cut and burn the dead. From the meadow, animals watched the destruction of their homes. They looked for new homes in the remaining woods. They were crowded and uncomfortable.

XIX.

In the fall, Big Deer returned to the Apple Tree for her delicious red apples. The apples were small, green and bitter that year. Big Deer was not satisfied. She did not have enough apple bits for a warm winter coat. All of the animals were hungry, weak, and cold that winter.

One day, as Big Deer and her Young Deer trudged through the snow in search of food, they came upon a patch of red blood. Big Deer sniffed and smelled her mate. She licked the red as if it were a wound, but tasted only snow. Sadly the deer walked on. Suddenly a gun shot exploded. The deer bolted. Big Deer headed for home, leading her young. Another shot rang out, closer still.

Big Deer stopped and cried to Young Deer, "Go on, it's safer separate. I'll return home later. Goodbye."

She bounded away in the opposite direction. Young Deer ran on. Finally, breathless, he reached the thicket where he waited for Big Deer's return. Dusk turned to starlight. Young Deer shivered, alone, but Big Deer did not come back.

In the morning, hungry and lonely, Young Deer set out to search for Big Deer and for food. He roamed far and wide until the sun was high in the sky. He found too little food and not a trace of Big Deer. When the sun began to sink, Young Deer turned for home. The woods were strange and unfamiliar. He could not find his way. He ran from one place to another hoping to find his path. He had no luck. He came to a strange meadow. Across the field, he saw another young deer. Young Deer was happy to see a New Deer like himself and ran towards him. The New Deer crouched as Young Deer approached.

" Are you a deer?" the New Deer called out.

"Yes, I am." Young Deer replied. "Let your senses tell you."

The New Deer sniffed Young Deer and said, "Yes, you are a deer. Come play with me."

The Young and the New Deer frolicked together, carefree in the snow.

From the woods a New Big Deer called, "New Deer, who is that with you?"

Young and New Deer approached her.

"This is my friend, Young Deer," the New Deer said to her mom, the New Big Deer.

"Are you alone?" New Big Deer asked Young Deer.

"Yes," Young Deer answered, "I lost my mom, Big Deer, after gunshots yesterday."

"You may stay with us," the New Big Deer said to Young Deer. "Now we must return to our thicket."

As they walked through the woods the New Big Deer pulled down tender branches from high in the trees for the New and Young Deer to eat. The new thicket was warm that night. As the winter passed Young Deer forgot his search for his Big Deer.

XX.

The snow melted and the spring rains came. The invasion of the colonial animalcule armies came to the crystals underground. Herbie Cide finally released R 'n A and D 'n A and hid in the cracks in the crystals. The Little Bits forgot about him when their Apple Tree's root pipes came to carry them up. Everyone except the Last Little Bit jumped on to the waiting tricycle at the door. She wanted to wait for flower time to go up so she could become Polli.

As the Bits rode up the tree they decided what jobs they wanted.

Red said to the driver, "I am tired of coming and going again and again. Is there a year round job?"

"Yes," said the driver, "you can be bark. You must bear the winter cold and wind, but you may stay in the tree year after year."

"That is perfect for me. I will stand strong and protect my tree forever. I want to be bark." The Pro Team driver stopped his tricycle half way up the trunk and dropped off Red.

"Here is a good place for you."

Red said goodbye to the other Bits, "Wave to me when you fall to the ground," and went to take his place in the bark.

When the rest of the Little Bits reached their new Island Green Leaf they were linked up by R 'n A and sent to their positions. Moli and Cule were back in a Sugar Factory. The Professor joined R 'n A, Sage T joined D 'n A, and the Delicious Guard became a Pro Team Driver. When everyone was settled into their jobs, it was flower time. The Last Little Bit came up, turned into a yellow Polli by R 'n A, and was sent to her stalk in the new flower.

XXI.

The aroma of the sweet nectar engulfed Polli as she waited for her magic carpet. At last, buzzing, the Honey Bee arrived and Polli was alight. They flew to flower after flower with colors and fragrances richer than she had ever known. In the late afternoon they approached a tiny new tree with a single bloom. They entered the flower. It was the most enchanting, inviting Polli to stay. She could not resist. She jumped from her magic carpet to the center of the flower. She slid down a rosy colored tube into euphoria. There she faced the most magnetic creature, The Egg.

The Egg said, "I am the Egg of the First Flower of the Young Tree grown from Little Baby Seed of Delicious Apple. Welcome to my chamber."

"I am Polli, the Last Little Bit of Delicious Apple.

"At last we are together" they said as one and embraced, never to part again.

They whirled and swirled and knew true love. United they grew together into a new apple. They became the first delicious apple of the new tree grown from Little Baby Seed of Delicious Apple of the Mother Apple Tree. And they lived happily ever after.

THE END

Annotated Glossary of characters and processes by chapters

II.

Dark Cave: Mouth

Clear juices: saliva

Soft moving floor: tongue

Pillars: teeth

Small tunnel: esophagus

Large hole: stomach

Juices: digestive juices

Squishing of tunnels: peristalsis

Mana Ure: manure

Last tunnel: intestines

III

Pro teams: proteins

Tricycles: Adenine Tri Phosphate, ATP, a molecule that stores and delivers energy

IV

Mighty Condra's Tricycle Factory: Mitochondrion, "The Powerhouse of the cell", a cell organelle where ADP, Adenine Di Phosphate, (a tricycle with a flat tire) is changed into ATP (Adenine Tri phosphate). Sugar is oxidized, or burned, and the energy is stored in a high energy phosphate bond. This is respiration:

$$ADP + O_2 + C_6H_{12}O_6 \dashrightarrow CO_2 + ATP + Heat$$

(Oxygen) (Glucose-Sugar)   (Carbon Dioxide)

R 'n A: RNA, Ribonucleid acid, the genetic material that

translates the genetic code from DNA into the proteins

and enzymes that are necessary for cell functioning and

growth

Scissors: jaws

Windows: eyes

Drum skin: ear drum

House: cell

Jelly: protoplasm

Work bench: Enzymes, holds molecules in place so they can

bond together

Pro Team messengers: The process by which most environmental

clues stimulate action or growth in plants and animals is not fully

understood. Protein like molecules, hormones and/or enzymes are

involved.

D 'n A: DNA, Deoxyribonucleic acid, the genetic code bearing

all the information for growth and operation of living

organisms

Inner chamber: Cell nucleus

Pro Tectors: Nuclear membrane, surrounds the nucleus

composed of protein and fat

VI.

Moli and Cule: a molecule, two bits of matter bonded together

Crystals: mineral component of soil

51

Pools: "soil water", attached to soil minerals (water is
also held by organic material, humus)

VIII

Colonial animalcules: Colonies of microorganisms (Anton Van
Leeuwenhoek discovered "animalcules using an early hand built
microscope

Round ones: cocci

Long tails: flagella

Nitro: <u>Nitrobacter,</u> a nitrifying soil bacteria

Actin: <u>Actinomycetes:</u> a fungal-like soil bacteria (these bacteria
change organic material in the soil into a form that
plants can use)

Sal: <u>Salmonella</u> bacteria

X

Chloro and Phyll's Sugar Factory: chloroplast, a cell organelle where chlorophyll, the light
absorbing pigment in green plants, is found. This is where the production of sugar using light
energy occurs. Sugar can be made into starches, cellulose, and part of DNA and RNA.

Guards: guard cells which open and close "stomata", leaf pores

Professor U: Uracil, U, one of the four "building block" nitrogenous base molecules that make up
the RNA chain

Sage T: Thymine, T, nitrogenous base that makes up DNA. A Sage is a wise person and an
herb used for tea.

R: messenger, m-RNA, which contains the code from a part of DNA for certain proteins

A: transfer, t-RNA, which matches amino acid molecules to the code in m-RNA, translating it into
actual proteins

XI

Magic Fairy Dust: the molecules in air

COO COO: CO_2, carbon dioxide

00: O_2, oxygen

HHO: H_2O, water

K bits: Potassium, K, found with sugar in high concentrations in the guard cells when open. Water flowing into areas of high concentration across a semi-permeable membrane is known as osmosis.

XII

HHO's stick together: cohesion

HHO's stick to the sides of the stream: adhesion

Both adhesion and cohesion of water are due to the

polar nature of the water molecule. Each molecule is like a magnet which attracts

the opposite pole of other water molecules. Many other molecules, the sides of the

stream, have a charge and will attract the water. Water moving up a narrow column

by adhesion and cohesion is known as capillary action. The mechanism by which sap

rises in a tree is not yet agreed upon, although capillary action contributes. Jagadis

Bose, an Indian scientist demonstrated a pulse in the sap which suggests heart-like

pumps in plants, perhaps regulated by electrical nerve impulses (discovered in

Nite11a plants by Drs. K.S. Cole and H.J. Curtis of Columbia University in 1938 as

reported in the New York Times)

XIV.

Light balls: Photons, particles of light Sugar made with light:

Photosynthesis

$$CO_2 + H_2O \text{ chlorophyll} \xrightarrow{\text{light}} C_6H_{12}O_6 + O_2$$

XV. Polli: pollen

XVI. A FID: an aphid

XVII. Herbie Cide: an herbicide, a man-made chemical used to kill vegetation.

XXI. Union of Polli and the Egg: genes from Pollen and an egg combine to form a new genetic mixture in a new seed. Technically, an apple must be pollinated with a different variety of apple. Also, it takes longer than two years for an apple seed to grow into a tree mature enough to develop a flower.

Made in United States
North Haven, CT
24 July 2022

21743668R00033